The KnowHow Book of Paper Fun

Usborne Publishing Ltd
20 Garrick Street
London WC2E 9BJ, England

© Usborne Publishing Ltd 1975

First published 1975
Seventh printing 1979
Eighth printing 1982

Printed in Italy

Published in Australia by
Rigby Limited
Adelaide, Sydney, Melbourne,
Brisbane, Perth

This abridged edition contains
the best projects from the
original 48-page version

About This Book

This is a book about all kinds of things to do and make with paper, from tricks with newspaper to paper flowers and paper sculpture. There are lots of big projects and some quick ones to do as soon as you take the book home. The projects at the beginning are easier to make than those at the end of the book.

For many of the projects all you need are paper, scissors, ruler and glue. Remember that the right kind of glue is important – use Bostik 1 or UHU. Page 32 tells you where to find special materials.

◎ Boxes with this sign give you special tips for making the projects work.

The KnowHow Book of Paper Fun

Annabelle Curtis and Judy Hindley

Illustrated by Colin King
Designed by John Jamieson

Educational Advisor: Frank Blackwell

Contents

Paper Tricks

Magic Ladder

1

Lay out two sheets of newspaper, like this, and roll them up. Fasten the ends with sticky tape.

2

Cut out the piece shown here. Throw this piece away.

3

Bend the roll back to make a bridge shape. Gently pull out the insides from each side. Here comes the ladder!

The more sheets of paper you use, the higher your ladder will go. Paper ladders can go as high as a two-storey house! (But you need strong hands to cut or tear through so much newspaper.)

Surprise Tricks

Twist a strip of paper and tape it into a loop. Put a red spot on the paper. Run your finger round and round the loop. Which is the inside of the loop?

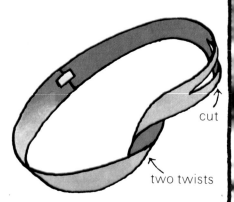

Now make a loop with two twists. Cut as shown to make two loops. Surprised?

Q: If you got lost in a blizzard with the Sunday papers, what would you do?

A: Cover your head and stuff your clothes with newspaper. Layers of newspaper trap thin sandwiches of air warmed by your body. (This is a real survival trick.)

Spray or paint the finished paper tree.

Wild Paper Tree

1 **2**

cut

tape

Roll up two sheets of newspaper as you did for the paper ladder. Tape as shown and make cuts about 15 cm long in the other end.

3 *pull up* **4**

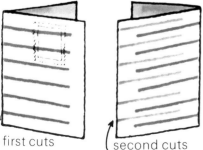

Now reach inside and gently pull the insides up and out.

Sitting Bird

1

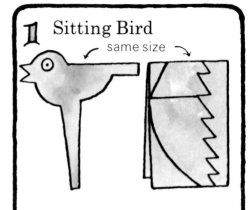

same size

Draw a long-legged bird on stiff paper and cut it out. Fold some paper and make a wing to fit the bird's back.

2

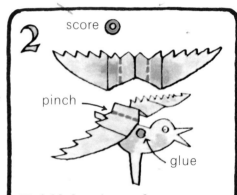

score

pinch

glue

Unfold the wing and score as shown. Fold each side towards the centre. Put glue on each side of the back, pinch on the wing and poke the leg into the top of the tree.

Walk Through a Postcard

unfold

first cuts *second cuts*

Fold the card. Make cuts from the fold almost to the edges. Now make another set of cuts from the edges almost to the fold. Don't cut through!

Open the card out and cut along the fold. But don't cut through the outside edges! Tug and see what happens.

How to Score

To score a straight line run the tip of your scissors along the paper against a ruler. Score curved lines without a ruler. Fold the paper firmly.

Pop-Up Cards

You will need
scissors and ruler
paints or crayons
pencil and glue
stiff paper

Fold carefully and crease hard
to make a pop-up card that really
pops. If you use very stiff paper,
it is a good idea to score the folds.
Remember – How to Score, p.5.

1 Ghost Pop-Up

Use a piece of paper twice as
long as it is wide. Fold in half
as shown. Then fold the top
corner from the centre fold to
the edge. Crease by folding
back and forth.

2

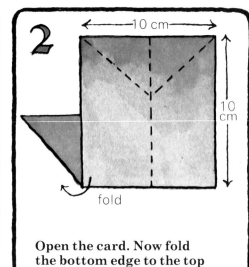

Open the card. Now fold
the bottom edge to the top
as shown.

3

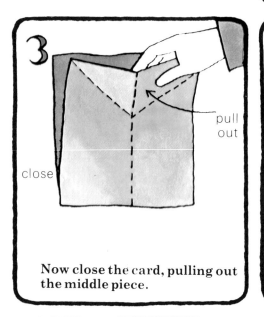

Now close the card, pulling out
the middle piece.

4

Cut off the top edge of the card.
When you open it again the
inside will pop up. Cut out and
decorate the pop-up.

◎ How to Mark a Straight Line

To cut paper the right size,
measure from the edge and
make a dot at the right number
of centimetres. Do this twice.
Draw a line through the dots
and cut this line.

Flying Witch

5 cm
30 cm
10 cm
15 cm

stick down

glue

Draw the back of a witch in the centre of the card. Then stick down a pleated strip of paper, measured as shown.

Dab glue on the pleat and close the card. Hold it shut till the glue is dry.

1 Horrible Spider Pop-Up

fold

10 cm

20 cm

10 cm

30 cm

Fold a piece of stiff paper in half. For the pop-up, use a piece half again as wide. Draw a long-legged spider on this piece.

2

turn under

Fold the pop-up as shown. Turn the outside edges under – these are the stick-on tabs. Now cut out the spider.

3

glue

glue

Glue the spider's feet to the inside of the card. Remember – the back of the folded spider must not stick out over the card edge.

Haunted House Peep-Show

Because of the way your eye works, paper figures can look mysteriously large and real when you squint at them through a peep-hole. Attach some of the figures to threads and pull-tabs and you can make a tiny theatre inside the box.

You will need
shoe box
tissue paper
stiff paper
ruler and scissors
needle and thread
glue and paints

How to Cut Panels

To start, turn the box so that the side you want to cut lies flat against something hard. Jab with the tip of the scissors. Pick it up again to finish.

Fix the Lid

cut

cover

dab glue

Cut panels in the lid. Dab glue around the panels on the inside and cover with tissue paper. Make small bats and spiders. Take a

needle and knotted thread, push through a bat, through the lid, and then through a paper stopper, to keep the bat dangling.

1 Fix the Box

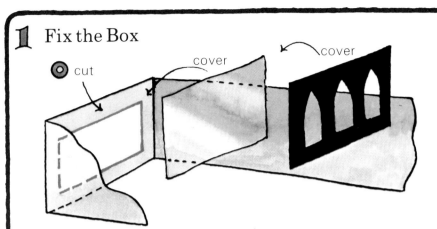

cut

cover

cover

Cut a panel from the back of the box. Turn it into a special window by covering first with tissue paper, then with cut-out paper. Now paint walls and floor.

2

hole

Make a small hole in the front and paint a scarey eye around it.

3

tab

feet tabs

Make stand-out figures and scenery with tabs on one side. Glue tabs to the side of the box. Make figures with tabs at the base to stand up in the middle of the box. They must all face forwards, tabs towards the back.

Action Figure – Prowling Monster

paper slide

Cut slots in the box and make a long slide of stiff paper. Glue the figure to it. Glue paper stops at the ends. Push back and forth.

Action Figure – Rising Spirit

glue tabs

cut and fold

knot

knot

To make the coffin, bend a strip of paper and stick down with tabs. Glue together at the ends. Then make a ghostly figure. Use needle and thread to make a cord that goes through the lid as shown. Pull and the spirit rises – let go and the spirit drops.

Mobiles

Blow on the mobile very gently to make it move. The balance is so delicate that it will move with currents of air that you don't even notice. Each hanging piece has a balance point and the arms of each move from side to side as well as up and down. Once you see how the balance works, you can invent new moving patterns.

You will need
wire or thin sticks
button thread (strong thread)
stiff paper and glue
scissors and needle

Balancing a Mobile

long arm   short arm

same length

same height

heavy weight

light weight

If both arms of a mobile are the same length, they balance equal weights. A short arm balances a heavier weight against a long arm.

move centre

When a mobile doesn't balance, move the centre thread very gradually towards the down end. Do this for each hanging piece.

1 Spinning Ball Mobile

cut two   cut

slot together

Slot two paper circles together as shown. String the models together with needle and thread and hang them from the wire.

2

wire

Lift by the top thread to balance. It may help to hang it from a coat-hanger hooked to the top of a door frame.

Lacy Lanterns

Folded paper is hard to cut through, so use the thinnest paper you can find. Make the cuts very deep and as close together as possible. When you first make the lantern it will be shaped like a flying saucer. As it hangs, it will gradually open up.

You will need
thin paper and scissors
string and glue
stiff paper for the base and top

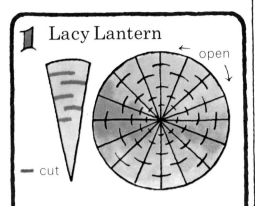

1 Lacy Lantern

cut

open

Cut two paper circles, using a big plate. Fold each in half four times. Then make very deep cuts from the sides as shown. Open flat.

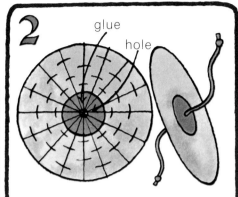

2

glue

hole

Glue small circles of stiff paper to the centre of each. When dry, make a hole in one of these and thread with string. Knot both ends.

Flying Fish Mobile

This pattern uses three balancing pieces. Make all the models first and lay the whole pattern flat on a table to fit together.

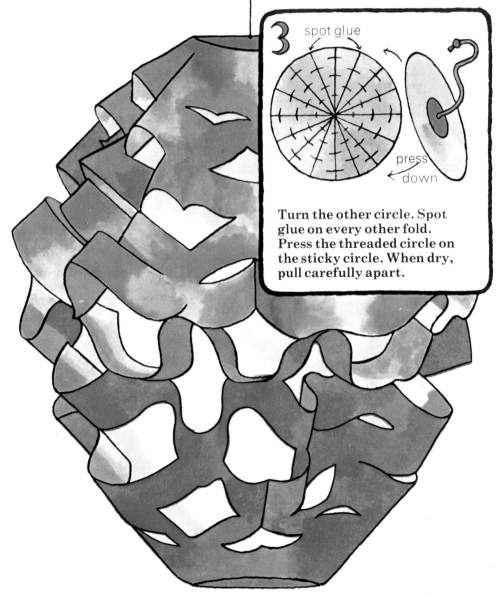

3

spot glue

press down

Turn the other circle. Spot glue on every other fold. Press the threaded circle on the sticky circle. When dry, pull carefully apart.

Paper Soldiers

You will need
stiff paper
ruler and scissors
pencil and paints
glue

Remember – use strong glue with a nozzle, so that you can dab spots of glue to add cut-out eyes, moustache, etc. Use a pencil end when your fingertips get sticky.

1 Paper Soldier

15 cm

15 cm

make cuts

For the body, make a roll of these measurements. Make cuts at the top. Paint the face and glue on eyes, moustache, etc.

2

bend and glue

Dab glue on the top strips. Bend one on top of another to make a dome shape.

How to Curl

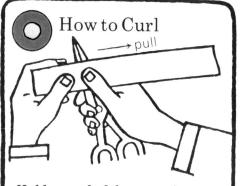

pull

Hold an end of the paper in one hand. With the other, hold it tightly between thumb and closed scissors and pull away with a quick, sharp movement.

5

6 cm

6 cm

cut

score inside

pinch

Make two rolls for the arms and glue one to the body. Cut the other as shown. Score it at the bend.

6

make two

2½ cm

Make hands and feet with tabs, from these patterns. Curl the hands.

Gluing Paper Sculpture

press with pencil

To glue a roll, press the join with a pencil held inside as shown. Use a pencil whenever you can't reach inside.

8

5 cm

10 cm

glue

glue

Make two rolls for the legs. Glue on the feet. Then make cuts as shown to slot the legs to the body.

9

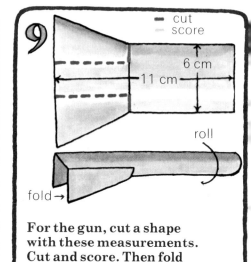

cut
score

6 cm

11 cm

roll

fold

For the gun, cut a shape with these measurements. Cut and score. Then fold and roll as shown.

3 mark and draw → cut

Hold a piece of paper around the body to make a cone shape and draw the jacket as shown. Then cut out the jacket.

4 — score   push down ↓

Cut and score the jacket neck as shown. Bend at the scored line to glue to the body. Join at back. Glue on a collar.

For the hat, glue a long strip of curled fringe round the head. Push down an extra bit of fringe.

7 glue →

Glue the bending elbow to the body and glue both hands to the arms.

Paper
People

KnowHow
Circle-Maker

3 cm   6 cm   9 cm

**Measure and punch holes in a
strip of cardboard. Stick
pencils through two holes.
Hold one pencil firm and
swing the other around.**

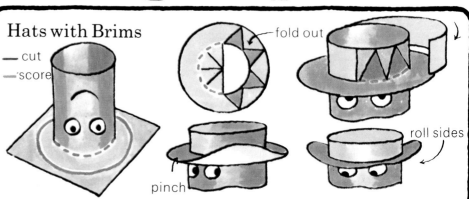

Hats with Brims

— cut
— score

fold out

pinch

roll sides

**Trace around the head and
score this mark. Then draw
a larger circle and cut it
out. Make cuts from the
centre to the scored line.**

**Push the head through the
centre. Glue a strip around
the top. Pinch front or roll
sides to make different brims.**

14

Faces

Glue on a cone nose, or cut and fold the shape shown. Glue big circles for eyes,

or roll a tiny strip and glue before sticking on. Add eyelashes and moustache.

Hair

cover

bald head

Cut and score a strip of paper as shown. Curl the bottom strips. Bend and glue

the top strips to the head. Cover with a circle, or stick paper curls all over.

Cone Hats

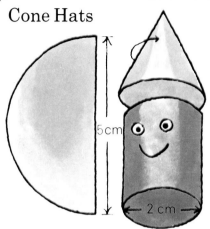

5 cm

2 cm

Make a semi-circle at least 2½ times as big across as the head. Use the KnowHow Circle-Maker. Roll into a cone and glue.

cut

cotton wool

For a Santa Claus hat, glue on cotton wool. For a Robin Hood hat, slice off the top. Make cuts in a feather shape and glue it on.

For finger puppets, make tubes that fit your fingers.

Paperville

Make a small house first, to see
how the pattern works. It's
easy to make if you start at
the edge of the paper and first
measure all the lines across,
then the lines going down.
Remember – How to Mark a
Straight Line, p.6.

You will need
large sheets of stiff paper
scissors, ruler
pencil, glue and paints

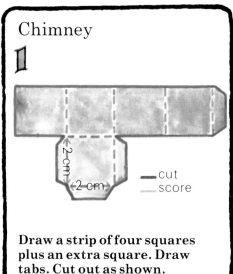

Chimney

1

2 cm

2 cm

━ cut
  score

**Draw a strip of four squares
plus an extra square. Draw
tabs. Cut out as shown.**

2

mark
━ cut
  score

**Hold next to the roof and
mark the shape on every
other square. Cut and score
both as shown and fold in
the triangles.**

House

1

measure in cm

Measure three lines from the side of the paper, like the red lines. Then start from the top and measure down to make five lines, like the blue lines.

2

— cut
— score

centre   throw away

base

1 cm tab

Draw lines from a centre point to the sides as shown. Draw tabs. Make doors and windows. Then score all round the base and along the tabs. Cut out.

3

6 cm

9 cm

Fold the tabs, fold up the house and glue. For a roof that just fits, fold paper measured as shown. Make it bigger to stick out.

3

Dab glue on the roof and fold the chimney round, using the folded triangles as tabs. Glue into a box.

4

— cut
— score

For a chimney pot, make a small tube. Cut and score one end to bend inwards and glue it to the chimney.

Making Boxes

base

— equal
— equal
— equal

You can make the basic box-shape as long or as tall as you like. But remember –
1. Make all the sides equal.
2. Make opposite sides of the base equal.

Paper Zoo

To make a stand-up animal, just cut the shape with its back along a fold. Then you can curl, glue and fold to make bending necks, curling tails and 3-D ears and wings. You will find patterns for all the animals on the next pages.

You will need

stiff paper
scissors and glue
paints or crayons to decorate
Remember – How to Score, p.5.
and How to Curl, p.12.

Stand-Up Deer — cut

1 Fold the paper and draw the deer with his back and neck along the fold.

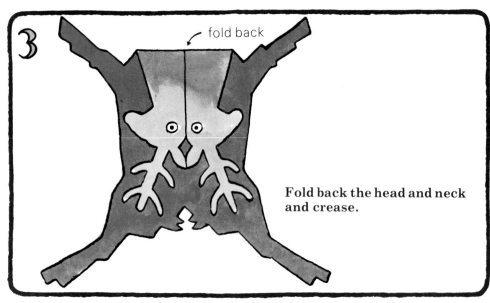

3 fold back

Fold back the head and neck and crease.

4 push down / push back.

Push the fold down and push the neck back as shown.

2

— score

Open flat and score as shown.

Paper Zoo Patterns

Piglet

curl

cut two

Cut ear shapes with a tab. Curl the ears and tail before gluing them on.

Mouse

push down

fold back

score

Fold and score as shown. Push down and back so that the mouse's head is tucked between its shoulders. Add a long curling tail. Hang by the tail.

Lion and Tiger

curl

cut two

For the lion's mane, cut a deep fringe in a strip of paper. Curl the fringe. Fold and glue on the neck.

Flapping Duck

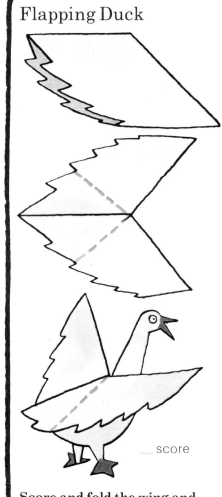

score

Score and fold the wing and glue it to the duck. If the duck is nose-heavy, put a very tiny bit of plasticine behind its tail.

Seal

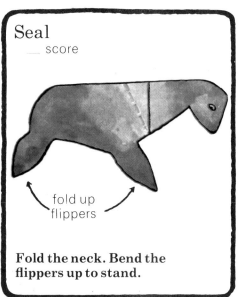

score

fold up flippers

Fold the neck. Bend the flippers up to stand.

Snake

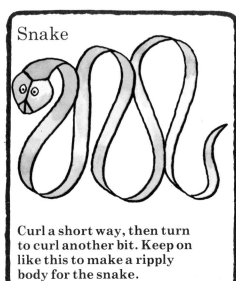

Curl a short way, then turn to curl another bit. Keep on like this to make a ripply body for the snake.

Giraffe

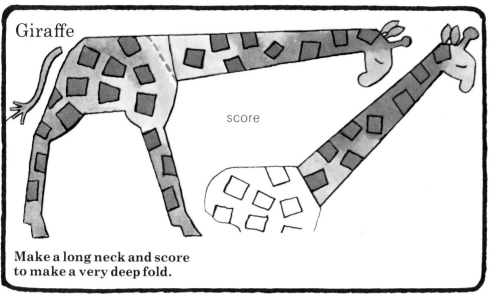

score

Make a long neck and score to make a very deep fold.

Duck and Chicken

score

Cow and Elephant

cut two

curl

Curl tusks before gluing on.

Pony

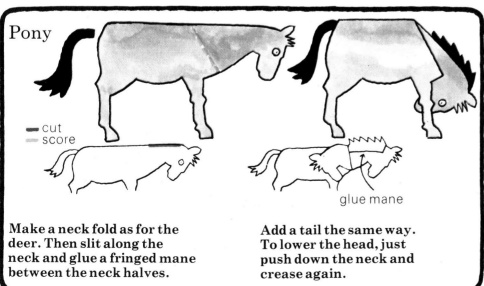

— cut
— score

glue mane

Make a neck fold as for the deer. Then slit along the neck and glue a fringed mane between the neck halves.

Add a tail the same way. To lower the head, just push down the neck and crease again.

Zebra

— cut
— score

The zebra is like the pony.

Castles and Things (1)

You will need

a large cardboard box
stiff paper
straws
glue and sticky tape
a paper fastener
silver foil
a cereal packet
a small pencil
a small strong cardboard box
cardboard
scissors
felt pens and paints

About Castles

On the right is a bird's eye view of the castle above. A soldier enters over the drawbridge and past the outer gatehouse or barbican. The land between the curtain wall and the keep is called the bailey. All the windows in the keep are very narrow. This makes it more difficult for an enemy's arrow to shoot in. On the next three pages you will find out how to make the keep and some of the things that go with it.

Battlements

Use a large cardboard box to make a keep. Cut battlements along the top. At each corner make a deeper cut.

1 To Make a Turret

Score and cut a tall sheet of stiff paper as shown. Decide how many turrets you want and do the same to each sheet. Draw some windows.

2

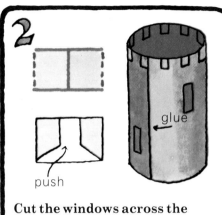

Cut the windows across the top, bottom and down the centre. Score the sides and push them in. Roll the turret up and glue.

3

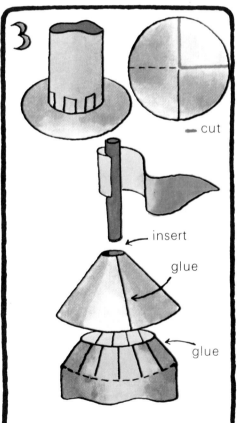

Cut a circle twice as wide as the tower and cut a piece out of it. Glue the rest into a cone. Glue a paper flag to a straw, snip off the top of the cone and push the straw in. Bend the cuts on the turret top inwards, dab on some glue and press the cone onto the turret.

Finishing the Keep

Hold a turret over a corner battlement and make two marks where it touches the keep. Cut two long slots from the two marks on the turret and push the turret onto the corner.

Curtain Walls

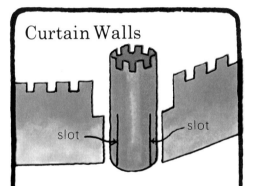

Cut battlements along the top of stiff paper with deeper cuts at each end. Cut two slots in each turret as shown and push the walls in. Make a line of walls.

1,500 Miles of Battlements

The Great Wall of China is so long that it is the only man-made building that can be seen from outer space.

Castles and Things (2)

The Drawbridge

Cut a door out of the wall. Glue card under the door, bend it up against the wall and make two holes above the door as shown. Thread string through the holes and knot.

1 The Rampart Walk

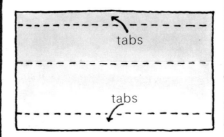

Cut out a piece of stiff paper wider than the box. Put the box on top and draw lines at both sides. Score and cut as shown.

2

Fold the paper like this. Glue the tabs to the keep just under the battlements. This is a rampart walk.

1 The Seige Tower

Siege towers are pushed up to the castle walls. The top door opens and out come the soldiers. First cut a cereal packet as shown.

2 For the Floors

Cut out a piece of stiff paper the same length as the keep wall. Score it as shown. The outer folds are the tabs.

Fold over the tabs and glue them into the box. Draw a ladder running up the inside. Make as many floors as you think it needs.

3 For the Door

Cut a door opening at the top of the tower. Use a paper fastener as a catch.

4 For the Wheels

Cut out two cardboard circles. Make holes in the centres. Tape a round pencil under the front end of the tower. Slot the wheels on. Crunch silver foil over the pencil ends.

5 Handles and Legs

Cut out two card handles and a card leg. Glue them onto the tower.

1 Making a Catapult

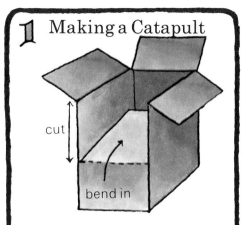

Cut half way down one side of a small strong cardboard box. Bend the flap inwards.

2

insert match

insert match

Make two holes with your scissors 2½ cm above the flap. Push the ends of a strong rubber band through the holes. Keep the band in there with matches.

3

tape

tape

Score and cut a small piece of card as shown. Tape the sides up and tape it to the end of a small pencil.

Push the catapult arm back. Put your ammunition in the ammunition holder, let the catapult arm go and fire.

4

Twist the rubber band round and round until you can't twist it any more. Push the catapult arm into its middle.

5

fold back top

Let the catapult arm spring up until it is pointing straight up. Fold back the top front flap and tape.

Paper Flowers

The stretchiness of crêpe paper is very useful. You can pull it into petal shapes or ruffled edges. With tissue paper you can show the vein of a leaf by making a lengthwise crease.

You will need
crêpe paper
tissue paper
sticky tape and scissors
strong glue with a nozzle
thin sticks or light wire (such as florist's wire or medium fuse wire) for the stems

Daisies

calyx
centre

Cut petals round a circle. Sandwich petals and stem between a centre circle and calyx shape and glue together.

Crêpe Paper Poppies

1

wind

For the centre, make cuts in a strip of paper as shown. Fasten it to the stem with thread, or glue the edge and wind it round and round.

2

Make eight petals. Cut them with the grain of the paper running up and down. Shape them by stretching sideways.

3

overlap

fold end of leaf

Glue the petals one by one around the stem. Then glue a long strip of paper under the flower and wind it down the stem, gluing in leaf shapes as you do so.

Tissue Paper Roses

1

loop

wind sticky tape

hole

Cut 16 circles of paper about 16 cm across. Make a wire stem as shown.

2

Turn upside-down and pinch the flower tightly round the stem as shown. Bind into shape with sticky tape.

3

calyx

Cut out a calyx. Slide it down the stem and glue it to the flower.

4

twist and fold

Turn the flower up again and shape it by pulling the petals out as shown. Twist and fold to make a centre. Cover the stem as before.

Carnations

1

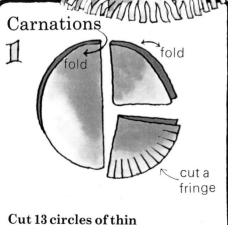

fold

fold

cut a fringe

Cut 13 circles of thin paper, about 9 cm across. Fold each into a quarter-circle. Make cuts as shown.

2

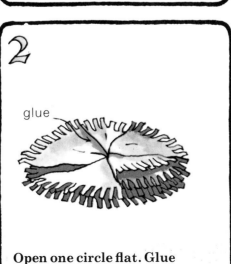

glue

Open one circle flat. Glue the quarter-circles onto it in layers as shown.

3

Loop the end of some wire and push it through to make a stem. Glue a strip of green paper round the stem.

Crocodile Marionette

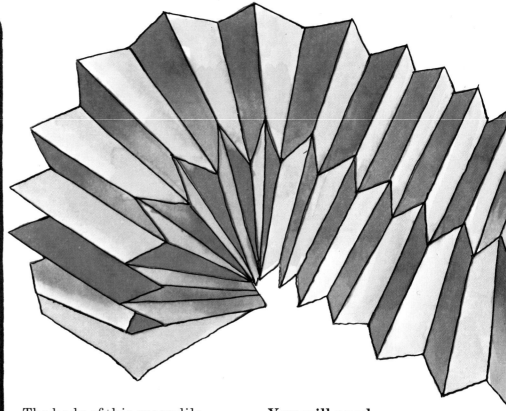

Paper Spring

1

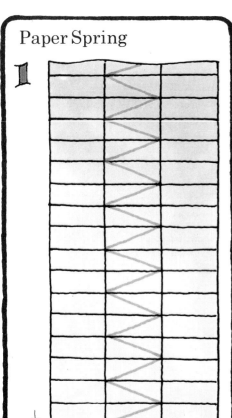

1½ cm

← 4 cm → ← 4 cm → ← 4 cm →

Use paper 12 cm wide and as long as possible. If you glue strips together, let the glue dry before you do the next step. Rule lines as shown and make a coloured zig-zag down the centre.

The body of this crocodile marionette is made from a strip of paper folded into a special spring. This makes a shape that can bend and twist and wriggle when you move the hanging strings. The fold is tricky until you get the knack, so follow the instructions carefully.

Remember – How to Mark a Straight Line, p.6.

You will need
coloured paper
ruler and scissors
glue and string
coloured pencil or felt pen
2 small sticks or rods

Turn the page to see how to make the head of the crocodile and how to work the strings.

2

Now make coloured lines joining the points of the zig-zag to the edges. Score all the coloured lines and crease them firmly.

3

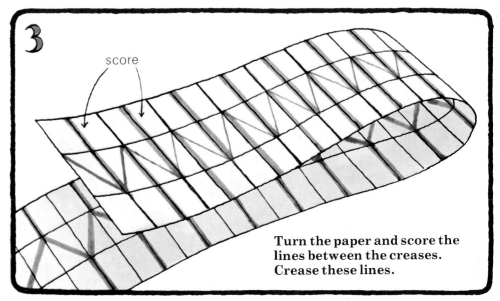

score

Turn the paper and score the lines between the creases. Crease these lines.

4 Hold the paper as shown. Walk your thumbs along the sides to push the creases inwards and pinch the folds between your fingers.

5 Continue until all the folds can be pinched between your fingers to make a shape like this.

Crocodile Marionette (2)

Make the Croc

1

cut

Take some paper about 40 cm long and 10 cm wide and fold in half. Draw and cut out the head shape.

2

score

glue teeth

glue tongue

Open and score as shown. Turn the head and glue strips of paper teeth inside the jaw.

Glue the end of a long tongue to the back of the top jaw.

3

push in

Now fold all the scored lines inward. Push in the crease between the V-shaped score at each side of the jaw.

4

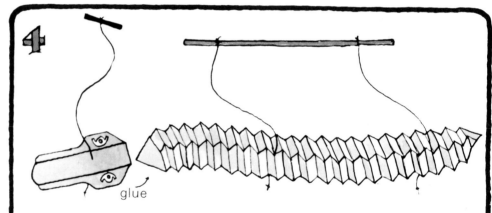

glue

Glue the paper spring to the back of the head. String up the crocodile with a needle and knotted thread as shown.

Tie the head string to a small stick. Tie the two back strings to another stick.

Work the Croc

Raise the head string to make the crocodile rear up and jerk the string to make its jaws open and close.

Rock the stick back and forth to make the crocodile hump its back as it moves along.

Hold your arms like this to make the crocodile turn and chase its tail.

Jack-in-the-Box

You will need
thin card for the box
coloured paper
ruler and pencil
scissors and glue

As you open the box, give it a
shake to make the Jack jump out.
If the Jack loses its spring
after a while, stretch it out and
fold it up again.
Remember — Making Boxes,
page 17.

1
glue

Make a paper spring 10 cm
wide and as long as possible.
Glue it to a head made from
a paper circle 10 cm across.

2
score

10 cm 10 cm 12 cm

put Jack here

12 cm 10 cm

Use the pattern shown to make
a box. Glue pieces with tabs
inside the box to hold the
Jack upright.

3
folded strip
paper slide
slotted strip

Fold a strip of paper and
glue it to the lid as shown.
Cut another strip with a
stand-up slot and glue it
to the front. Lock the box
with a slide of stiff paper.

Tips on What to Use

Here are some suggestions to help you find the right materials for the projects.

Canes and Florists' wire — Buy at a gardening shop or at a florist's.

Cold-water paste — Buy Rex Cold-water Paste at an art supply shop or buy wallpaper paste at a hardware shop. Wallpaper paste is not a good thing to get in your mouth, so be sure to wash your hands when you have used it.

Glue — Use strong glue with a nozzle, like Bostik 1 or UHU.

Fuse wire — Buy at Woolworth's.

Medium galvanized wire — Buy at Woolworth's.

Sticky tape — Use Scotch Tape, if you can find it. It's very strong and doesn't split.

Stiff coloured paper — You can buy it in sheets at an art supply shop. Ask for cartridge paper. It can be light or heavy, so be sure to say what you want it for.

Thin paper — Buy at an art supply shop. Ask for a layout pad or for sheets of detail paper.

Cartridge paper and detail paper are sold in packets at many stationery shops, but the sheets are too small for several of the projects.

Did You Know?

You can buy paper that is strong enough to bear the weight of a car.

Did you Know?

Up to 20 miles of paper can be produced every hour by a large papermaking machine.